The Baby Sleep Book

Top 250+ Essential Tips To Get Your Baby
To Sleep Through The Night
And Find a Permanent Solution
To Your Child's Sleeping Problems

by Sarah Jefferson

Contents

About This Book

I come from a family of insomniacs. When I was growing up, sleep was an obsession in my family. It was the holy grail: you'd never, ever wake someone up unless the house was burning down.

As a baby, I was a terrible sleeper who cried for hours on end until deep into the night. My parents did everything to get me to sleep - rocking, driving around, and letting me share their bed. When I grew into an adult, I still suffered from insomnia but I managed to deal with it... until I fell pregnant.

I was terrified of what my baby would do to my precious sleep. So I started devouring books, magazine articles, and the Internet for information on baby sleep. I spent many hours reading all the pros and cons of controlled crying, co-sleeping, and strict routines. I was determined to get my baby to sleep and devised a battle plan based on what I'd read.

To my surprise, my first baby Ava was a pretty good sleeper. When she was eight weeks old, I still clearly remember waking up in the morning, wondering why I felt so refreshed. Then it dawned on me: I hadn't fed Ava in the middle of the night. Thinking the worst must have happened, I raced to her bedroom to find her blissfully asleep. She had slept through the night!

It came to me as a shock when my second baby was born. Jackson turned out to be more like me, crying for hours on end, and did not settle down unless he was fed or rocked to sleep. I had no choice but to dig up my old research on sleep.

I did some experiments and ended up with a mixture of the major theories. I let Jackson sleep in a darkened room, swaddled him, put him into a flexible routine, used some controlled crying on him as well as patting him to sleep, and even tried co-sleeping (not recommended for insomniacs!). Eventually, I found out what techniques worked for him. His sleep improved: he was sleeping through the night at six months and had solid naps during the day.

From my experiences and talking to other parents, I realized that what works for one baby doesn't necessarily work for another. Babies have different temperaments, and parents have different views on how to care for their babies.

This book is a compilation of sleep tips from my research on baby sleep. Contrary to other baby sleep books, it doesn't prescribe any particular method or technique. You are free to pick and choose from these ideas and experiment to find out what works for you and your baby.

Wishing you the best of luck in your sleeping journey,

Sarah

Email: sarahjeffersonbooks@gmail.com
Website: www.sarahjeffersonbooks.blogspot.com

CHAPTER ONE

Rule Out Conditions That May Affect Your Baby's Sleep

1 - Your baby's sleep will be affected if she is suffering from medical conditions; confirm this with your doctor. Do not start any type of sleep training until you are certain that your baby is completely healthy. Examples of medical conditions affecting sleep are:

- acid reflux
- food allergies and sensitivities (watch what you're eating and drinking when you're breastfeeding)
- environmental allergies, e.g. a dust-mite allergy
- sleep apnea
- anaemia
- fevers, colds, and ear infections

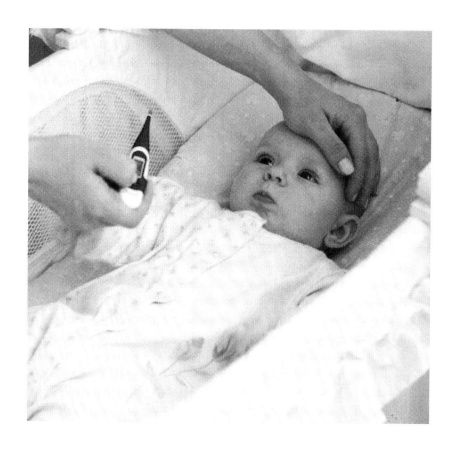

2 - When babies reach developmental milestones such as sitting or crawling, they may wake up at night and practice their new skills. Give them plenty of exercise time during the day.

3 - When your baby goes through a growth spurt, this may affect her night-time sleep. Be patient; a growth spurt is only temporary.

4 - Under- or overfeeding could also cause sleep problems. If you're breastfeeding, don't switch breasts too early and try to get your baby to get to the filling hind milk. Check her weight regularly.

5 - If your baby is uncomfortable in any way, for example if she's too hot or cold, in a noisy environment or has a nappy rash, she won't be able to sleep. See Make Your Baby Feel Comfortable for tips on making your baby comfortable.

6 - Teething causes babies discomfort, and will affect sleep. Teething gels may help, or in serious cases, Tylenol/paracetamol. Check with your doctor first.

7 - Babies will have more trouble sleeping when they do not follow a routine. Read more about routines in 'Develop a Sleeping Routine'.

8 - If you miss a baby's signs of being tired and don't put her to bed early enough, she may become overtired and find it hard to fall asleep. Read more about tired signs in 'Get To Know Your Baby's Tired Signs'.

9 - Babies up to about three to four months occasionally stretch their arms and legs out during sleep and may wake themselves up (the Moro reflex). It would help to swaddle or wrap your baby (see 'Make Your Baby Feel Comfortable').

10 - From around six months, your baby may start suffering from separation anxiety. Give her opportunities to be by herself during the day, and keep on assuring her that you are nearby.

11 - Some babies are just better sleepers than others. Highly sensitive, alert, and active babies have more trouble falling asleep. Find a sleep method and routine that works for you and your baby (refer to the chapters 'Find a Sleep Method That Suits You and Your Baby' and 'Develop a Sleeping Routine').

12 - Babies are sensitive beings, and any stress in the family may disturb their sleep. Try to limit the stress as much as you possibly can. This is not a good time to start sleep training.

CHAPTER TWO

Find the Quickest Way for Your Baby To Fall Asleep

13 - Try different ways of getting your baby to fall asleep. Find out which ways are always successful, and which are the fastest. (Note: many sleep experts advise against these quick fixes as a baby may become dependent on them to fall asleep. To find a long-term sleep solution, read 'Find a Sleep Method That Suits You and Your Baby'.)

14 - Breast- or bottle feed your baby to sleep.

15 - Give him a dummy/pacifier.

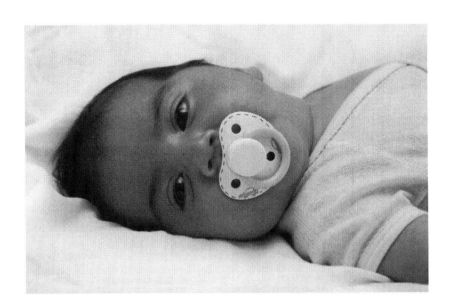

16 - Rock him to sleep in your arms.

17 - Roll your baby to his side; hold his shoulder with one hand and pat him rhythmically on the bottom with the other, cupped hand.

18 - Place him in a rocker or recliner and gently rock him.

19 - Try a baby hammock or swing, and gently swing him from side to side.

20 - Place him over your shoulder while pacing up and down.

21 - Take your baby for a ride in the car.

22 - Go for a walk with the pram or stroller.

23 - Put baby in a baby sling or carrier.

24 - Hold your baby while you gently bounce on a balance ball.

25 - Play sleepy music (see also 'Play Soothing Sounds and Music').

26 - Gently jiggle the bassinet, pram, or stroller. Make sure your baby's head wobbles only slightly.

27 - Wheel your pram or stroller backwards and forwards. Riding over a slight bump may also help.

28 - Softly shake the mattress your baby's lying on without touching him.

29 - Snuggle up to baby in bed. Make sure baby is safe from any hazards, see also 'Co-Sleeping or Bed Sharing'.

30 - Stroke him gently on his forehead down the bridge of his nose; in the first two months this triggers a reflex that causes sleepiness.

31 - Sing when your baby is falling asleep in your arms, and put him to bed while continuing to sing.

32 - Place him on his side, place your hands on his shoulder and hip, and rock him gently backwards and forwards.

33 - Put your hands on his shoulder and bottom and say 'ssshhh'. Slowly lighten your hands and take them off one by one when he is asleep.

34 - Place your wrapped baby on your lap, with his feet towards you. Gently jiggle him from side to side with your knees.

35 - Do any of the above accompanied by soothing music or sounds, or your quiet, calm voice.

CHAPTER THREE

Make the Baby Room Comfortable

36 - Take all the necessary safety precautions, like making sure the cot or crib meets all safety standards, placing it away from any lights, cords, or windows, and checking for gaps between mattress and frame.

37 - Keep your baby's bedroom dark. Babies who are sensitive and easily stimulated sleep better in pitch-black darkness. Use block-out curtains or blinds.

38 - Make sure the baby bedroom is as quiet as possible.

39 - For extra sensitive babies, play white noise to block out any sounds (see 'Play Soothing Sounds and Music').

40 - Keep the temperature between 66 and 72°F, or 19 and 22°C .

41 - Check the humidity level in the room. If it's too humid, you will find moisture running down the windows. If it's too dry, you will experience the effects of static electricity, like static electric shocks. You can also use a hygrometer (found at hardware stores), and keep the humidity at 50%.

42 - Dim the light for night feedings. You could also use a small lamp or night light.

43 - Use a comfortable, firm mattress.

44 - Before you put your baby to bed, warm her bedsheets by putting them in a tumble dryer.

45 - Heat the sheets briefly with a warm hairdryer. Check the temperature with your hand.

46 - Place baby's sheets in a bed heated by an electric blanket. Do not use an electric blanket in her bed.

47 - Heat up the sheets with a hot water bottle. Remove the hot water bottle before putting baby into bed.

48 - When the weather is hot, place the sheets in the fridge or put a cold water bottle in the cot.

49 - If your baby uses dummies or pacifiers, scatter these around the cot for nighttime comfort.

50 - Play a slide show or screensaver on your computer, laptop or tablet, accompanied by soothing sounds or music.

51 - Make your baby's bed a restful place. Don't put stimulating toys like mobiles above the bed.

52 - Put a drop of lavender or chamomile oil on the carpet or curtain in baby's room, for a restful effect.

53 - Make the bedroom dust-free, for instance with a HEPA air filter. This is especially important for babies with dust-mite allergies.

54 - Make your baby feel safe in her cot or crib. Let him spend some enjoyable quiet time there during the day - reading, playing, and talking.

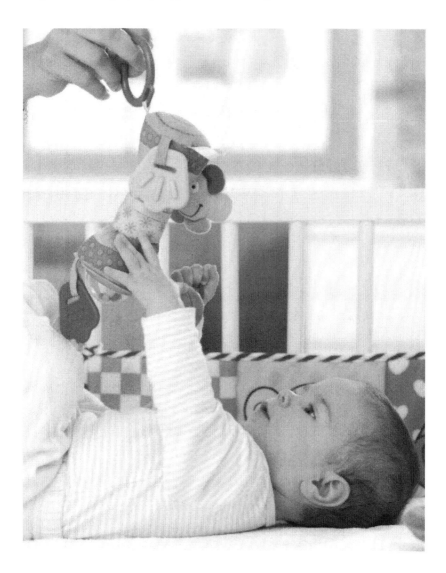

55 - Place a comfortable chair (rocking chair), a book, and a drink of water next to baby's bed to make night feeds more comfortable.

56 - Put a CD player in the room. See 'Play Soothing Sounds and Music' for music and sound suggestions.

57 - Place a laptop or tablet in the room that plays music as well as a slideshow or screensaver, for example of fish.

CHAPTER FOUR

Make Your Baby Feel Comfortable

58 - Swaddle or wrap your baby to prevent him waking up from the startle or Moro reflex. For instructions on how to swaddle, see **http://bit.ly/XPqEqV**.

59 - When he is three to four months, leave one or two arms out of the swaddle so can reach his hands to soothe himself.

60 - When your baby is getting too big for swaddling, dress him in a sleep-suit or sleeping bag with the right TOG or warmth rating:
- 0.5 TOG: hot weather (24-27°C or 75-81°F)
- 1.0 TOG: warm weather (20-23°C or 69-73°F)
- 2.5 TOG: winter/cold weather (16-20°C or 61-69°F)

61 - Use only soft cotton clothing and bedding, making sure nothing is scratchy or itchy.

62 - Try different types of dummies or pacifiers to find the one your baby likes best.

63 - Help your baby put his thumb or fist to his mouth to suck on and soothe himself.

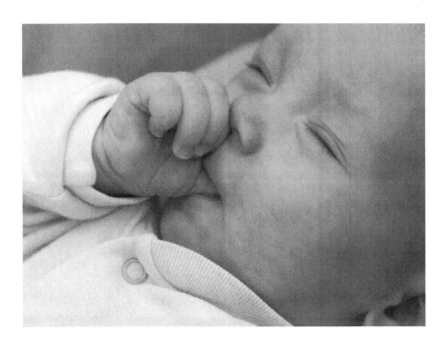

64 - Give him a warm bath (around 100°F/38°C) before sleep. You can add a drop of lavender oil in the water, which is said to have a calming effect.

65 - Instead of a baby bath, you could also give your baby a deep bath in the adult bath.

66 - If you have to change soiled or very wet diapers at night, use warm wipes.

67 - When it's hot, wet your baby's face with a cool face washer and offer cool water.

68 - When your baby has a stuffy nose or is suffering from reflux, prop up the mattress on one side by placing a pillow or blanket underneath it, or phone books under two legs of the bed or cot.

69 - Introduce a small comfort object (make sure it is not floppy and has no small removable pieces including clothes) or special blanket that your baby will associate with sleep. Leave it in his cot when he's around six months and no longer swaddled or wrapped.

70 - Put an object with your smell in your baby's bed. You could transfer your scent to his sheets, wrap, blanket, or comfort object by carrying it around or sleeping with it.

71 - Give him a full-body massage from the top of his head to his toes. See **http://bit.ly/11uqsa** for an instructional video.

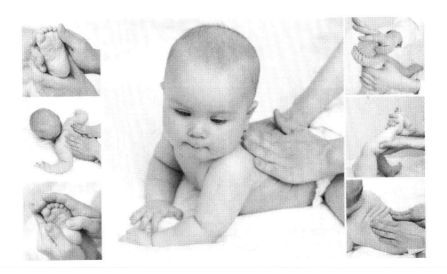

CHAPTER FIVE

Play Soothing Sounds and Music

72 - Sing songs or lullabies to get her ready for sleep. Even if you don't like your own voice, your baby will always be your biggest fan.

Hush-a-bye don't you cry,
Go to sleep-y, little baby.
When you wake you shall have
All the pretty little horses.
Blacks and bays, dapple grays,
Coach and six white horses.
Hush-a-bye don't you cry,
Go to sleep-y, little baby.

73 - Talk to your baby in a soft, gentle voice when it's time for bed.

74 - Make a shushing sound (ssshhh, ssshhh, ssshhh). You could do this in combination with rocking or jiggling.

75 - Play Brahms' *Lullaby*, Beethoven's *Moonlight Sonata*, Mozart, or other classical music. Make sure the music has an even pitch without sudden spikes.

76 - Play music and songs with simple rhythms and repeating words, not complex (classical) music.

77 - Place a fish tank in the room with a bubbling water filter.

78 - Play TV or radio static.

79 - Try soothing new age music.

80 - Find Internet radio stations on your phone, tablet, or computer that broadcast sleep sounds, like **tunein.com** (search for 'sleep') or **8tracks.com/explore/sleep**, or try white noise websites, like **simplynoise.com** or **rainymood.com**.

81 - Play soundscapes like waves crashing against the rocks, or a soft breeze through the leaves in a forest. Download your bonus waves MP3 - read 'A Gift from Me'.

82 - Play sounds mimicking the heartbeat.

83 - Read poetry or rhymes.

84 - Try out talking storybooks.

85 - Hang wind chimes in front of an open window.

86 - Play music from a jewelry box.

87 - Place a water feature in the room that makes the sound of running water.

88 - Play the sound of running bathwater.

89 - Reverse a baby monitor so your baby can hear you in the other side of the house.

90 - Place a ticking clock in the room.

91 - Leave the bedroom door open so your baby can hear normal household noise.

92 - Recreate familiar sounds of pregnancy, like the clicking sounds of a computer keyboard.

93 - Play recorded white noise sounds, for instance a washing machine, dryer, dishwasher, microwave, vacuum cleaner, electric fan, or exhaust fan.

94 - Record your voice - talking, singing or shushing - and play this after you leave the room.

CHAPTER SIX

Get To Know Your Baby's Tired Signs

95 - Observe your baby's behavior and try to read her tired signs. All babies are different and show different signs of being sleepy.

96 - Check the time your baby has been awake to be able to predict when she's tired. Use the following awake times as a guideline:

- 2 to 6 weeks: 1 to 1¼ hours
- 6 weeks to 3 months: 1 to 2 hours
- 3 to 6 months: 1½ to 2½ hours
- 6 to 9 months: 2 to 3 hours
- 9 to 12 months: 3 to 4 hours

97 - Look out for signs that babies of all ages may show when they are tired, like:

- frowning
- yawning
- clenching fists
- grizzling
- staring
- rubbing eyes
- keeping limbs rigid
- sucking fingers
- poor feeding

98 - From birth to three months, you will know that your baby is tired when she is:

- whining, developing into crying, and screaming
- showing a glazed stare
- looking away
- turning head away
- arching back

- frowning or grimacing with eyes closed and mouth open
- clenching fists tightly
- pulling knees up
- waving arms and legs
- jerking arms and legs
- sucking

99 - Babies three to six months show the following signs:

- whining, crying, and screaming
- having a glazed stare
- looking away
- turning head away
- back arching
- losing interest in toys and playing
- pulling ears or hair
- sucking fingers
- rubbing eyes or nose
- yawning
- being clingy
- becoming moody
- having temper outbursts

100 - Tired signs in babies six to 12 months include:

- all the above signs of the three- to six-month olds
- being disinterested or bored with toys
- concentrating less
- needing constant entertaining
- needing more physical contact
- being clumsy

101 - When your baby starts crying and screaming, she is already overtired. Overtired babies are difficult to get to sleep and wake easily. Try to calm her down first before trying to get her to sleep.

102 - Be aware that a lot of babies do not yawn when they are tired. Check carefully for other tired signs like eye-rubbing, even if your baby does it only once for a split second.

103 - Be very alert if you have a very active baby as it will be more difficult to recognize her tired signs. It is probably easiest to check the time she has been awake to figure out when she is tired.

104 - Put your baby down on the floor or in her playpen to spot her tired signs as you are likely to miss these signs when she is in your arms.

105 - Once she is displaying any signs of being tired, slow things down and get her ready for bed.

106 - When a baby is about to fall asleep, she will show the following signs:

- a relaxed body
- fluttering eyelids
- sobbing
- sighing
- hums and groans

CHAPTER SEVEN

Find a Sleep Method That Suits You and Your Baby

107 - Find out which settling method or technique you're comfortable with. All methods work, but not necessarily for all babies. It may require trial and error to find out a way that works for you and your baby.

108 - Choose from these main methods or techniques: sleep training or controlled crying; co-sleeping or attachment parenting; and supported self-settling.

109 - Here is the difference between good and poor sleepers. All babies come into a light sleep after completing a sleep cycle. Good sleepers can put themselves back to sleep but poor sleepers wake up fully and need help getting back to sleep.

110 - Co-sleepers would feed or cuddle babies back to sleep, while sleep trainers would expect them to go back to sleep by themselves through controlled crying. Supported sleep settlers would help babies fall asleep initially, but expect them them to sleep by themselves eventually.

111 - If you believe that sleep is a learned skill and that parents can create positive sleep associations to help a baby fall sleep by himself, you should consider sleep training or supported self-settling.

112 - If you feel that a baby should fall asleep by your side, without any crying, then co-sleeping and attachment parenting will suit you best.

113 - To read more about sleep training and controlled crying, turn to Dr. Marc Weissbluth, Dr. Richard Ferber, and Jodi Mindell.

114 - Attachment parenting, co-sleeping, and bed sharing is advocated by Dr. Benjamin Spock, Elizabeth Pantley, Sheila Kitzinger, and Dr. William Sears.

115 - If you're interested in supported self-settling techniques, read Tracy Hogg, Sheila Kitzinger, Dr. William Sears, and Dreena Hamilton.

116 - For routines and discipline, read Jodi Mindell, Gina Ford (for strict routines), Dr. Richard Ferber, Dr. Marc Weissbluth, and Tracy Hogg.

117 - Follow your instincts and choose a method or technique you feel comfortable with. If you feel it's wrong in some way, or it makes you feel guilty, stop immediately. Take a break before you try something different.

118 - Make a decision together with your partner. You'll need his or her support to be able to succeed.

119 - Once you've picked a sleeping method that you're comfortable with, persist with it. Give it at least one week. A sleep log or diary will show if your baby's sleeping has improved after a week. See 'A Gift from Me' for a printable sleep log.

120 - Be consistent. Stick to the method you've chosen, and don't revert to your old method when the going gets tough. If your baby gets confused by these mixed messages, the new method is not likely to work.

121 - Spend time watching and listening to your baby when he is asleep to familiarize yourself with the noises and movements he makes during sleep. This prevents you from being overly worried when trying new sleeping methods.

122 - Find out what your baby's crying means:
- whining, fussing: not very upset
- rhythmic, repetitive cry: hungry
- loud, prolonged cry: angry, fed up
- sudden high-pitched scream: in pain
- screaming, accompanied by sweating, a red face, and a frantic look: distressed

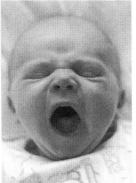

123 - Remember, each baby and each mother is unique. What works for your friends and their babies may not work for you.

124 - Celebrate any small progress. Even if your situation is far from perfect, it is better than before.

125 - Be realistic about sleeping through the night. Sleep researchers define it as a five- to six-hour stretch.

Sleep Training or Controlled Crying

126 - Sleep training or controlled crying involves leaving your baby in a room to sleep by herself and letting her cry for a certain amount of time before going back to settle her.

127 - A sleep-trained baby will be able to fall asleep by herself with no or minimal crying.

128 - Try sleep training or controlled crying only when your baby is six months or older.

129 - Start the training when your schedule is free from any appointments, parties or holidays, and when you know you can see it through.

130 - Stay at home during the training period.

131 - You'll have to set aside at least three or four days for this method to start working.

132 - Make sure your baby is completely healthy and not affected by any medical or other conditions (see 'Rule Out Conditions That May Affect Baby's Sleep').

133 - Before you start, get your baby used to short periods of separation.

134 - Make her cot or crib a peaceful, enjoyable place. You could read to her and let her play in her cot during the day.

135 - Inform neighbors and other house members of what you are doing, and assure them it will only be temporary.

136 - To start training, say goodnight to your baby and leave her in her room to sleep. When she starts crying, go back into the room after 3, 5, 10, 15, and 20 minutes, and continue going back every 20 minutes until your baby is asleep.

137 - You could also try 2, 4, 6, 8, and 10 minutes, and go back every 10 minutes.

138 - Use a timer. You'll become a poor judge of time once your baby starts crying.

139 - When you go back into the room, give your baby brief comfort. Tell her you love her and stroke her on the cheek. Do not feed, rock, pat, pick up, or change her position.

140 - For this method to work faster, use it for all sleeps - naps as well as nighttime sleep.

141 - Keep a chart to record progress.

142 - Be consistent in following the method at all times and do not fall back to your old method. This will give your baby mixed messages, and sleep training will probably be unsuccessful.

143 - Stop training when your baby is unwell, and start again when she is completely recovered.

144 - Be aware that it will be harder and take longer to sleep-train older babies.

145 - Show confidence and joy when leaving your baby alone, not insecurity or fear as she will be able to pick up your feelings.

146 - Keep the goal in mind: after training, your baby will become an independent sleeper with no or minimal crying.

147 - Stop this method if your records do not show any progress after one week even though you have been consistent carrying it out.

148 - Do not try this method if:
- you feel it's wrong somehow
- your partner doesn't support you
- your living situation doesn't allow it, e.g. if you have thin walls or are sharing your home

Co-Sleeping or Bedsharing

149 - Before you start sharing your bed with your baby, take precautions to keep him safe.

150 - Use the biggest bed possible. Here are some ideas:
- Turn the bed around so the length becomes the width of the bed.
- Put two beds together, like a queen and a single.
- Buy a king size bed.

151 - Put the bed against the wall.

152 - Remove any potential dangers, like cutouts in the headboard where baby's head could get stuck.

153 - Use a firm mattress. Do not co-sleep in a waterbed, especially one that is wavy.

154 - Make sure there are no gaps between the mattress and the wall. Fill these up with rolled-up towels if necessary.

155 - Place rugs or pillows around the bed.

156 - For further safety, you could also place mattresses on the floor.

157 - Place a snuggle bed or small mattress for your baby on top of your bedding.

158 - Use a sidecar cot or bassinet next to your bed, which could be open to the parents' side.

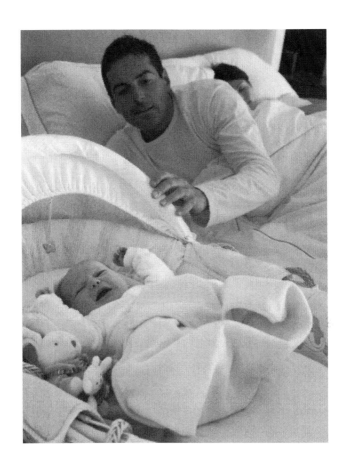

159 - Use traditional sheets and blankets rather than duvets or comforters.

160 - Pillows also cause a hazard to a young baby, so remove them and other objects from the bed.

161 - It's safest to let baby sleep between his mother and the wall.

162 - If your baby is sleeping between you and your partner, let baby sleep on a small mattress.

163 - Pull your hair back and fasten it.

164 - Keep the sleep area free from strong smells like hairsprays, deodorants, or perfumes.

165 - Do not wear any dangling jewelry or string ties.

166 - Only sleep with your baby when you're completely sober. Do not drink any alcohol, take drugs or sleeping pills, or smoke cigarettes.

167 - Make sure your baby is not overdressed.

168 - Do not swaddle or wrap your baby.

169 - Let older siblings share the bed only when the baby is six months or older.

170 - Do not let pets sleep in the bed.

171 - Find the most comfortable position for feeding and sleeping. You may want to keep your baby in the crook of your elbow with his head resting on your arm.

172 - Co-sleep only in bed. Do not sleep with your baby on a couch or sofa, beanbag, recliner, or armchair as he could easily get stuck in gaps.

173 - Face your baby when you're sleeping.

174 - If you'd like to have the bed to yourself once in a while, you could try an occasional family bed where the baby alternates between your bed and his own cot or crib.

175 - You could also use two beds, one to share with your baby and one with your partner.

176 - Some families prefer not to have fixed sleeping places and move from bed to bed, and room to room, whenever they feel like it.

177 - Co-sleeping is not suitable for highly active, constantly moving or very independent babies.

Supported Self-Settling

178 - Supported self-settling involves actively helping babies fall asleep by themselves with the least possible crying. Babies wake up at the same place that they fell asleep, which means that they are more likely to doze off again at the end of a sleep cycle, instead of constantly waking through the night.

179 - Get baby to sleep in her own room from birth. Even if your baby sleeps with you, get her used to being in her own room for short periods.

180 - Settle her in her cot or crib at night and for most day sleeps.

181 - Try to keep your baby awake after daytime feeds.

182 - If she falls asleep straight after the last feed of the day, arouse her slightly before settling her in the cot or crib. If you're breastfeeding, break the suction with your little finger.

183 - To start supported self-settling, carefully watch for tired signs. Read 'Get To Know Your Baby's Tired Signs'.

184 - When your baby is showing signs of being tired, settle her with whatever method works best, like feeding, giving her a dummy or pacifier, rocking or patting (see also 'Find the Quickest Way for Your Baby To Fall Asleep'). But do not let her fall asleep.

185 - Place your baby in her cot or crib when she is drowsy but still awake. If you're using a dummy or pacifier, remove it before she falls asleep.

186 - Sit next to her, and stroke, rub, sing, or talk to her but don't pick her up.

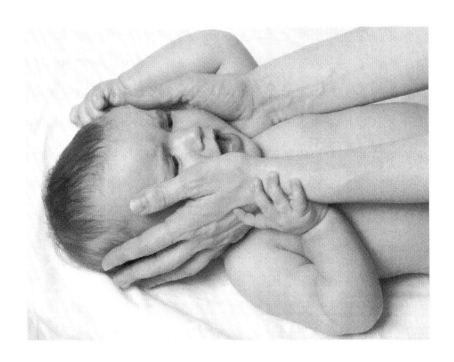

187 - If your baby is unsettled, use your best method to settle her down and put her down sleepy but not asleep. Repeat until she falls asleep.

188 - Once your baby falls asleep, wait five to 20 minutes for her to reach the deep sleep stage when she is motionless and breathing deeply.

189 - When you are successful getting your baby to fall asleep using the above tips, you could try to leave the room instead of sitting next to her when she is settled in her cot or crib.

190 - If your baby starts crying, listen to her crying sounds:

- whining, fussing, with pauses: not very upset
- loud, prolonged cry: angry, fed up
- screaming, accompanied by sweating, a red face, and a frantic look: distressed

191 - Go back into the room before your baby is distressed. Don't look at the clock or use a timer. Keep in mind that babies cry to get attention only from eight to nine months old.

192 - Calm her down again until she's sleepy. Leave the room and repeat if necessary until your baby is asleep.

193 - For babies who need more help in settling, create positive sleep associations that help them fall asleep, like music, toys, lullabies, or special sleep words (e.g. 'it's time for sleep now'). You only use them when it's time for bed so that your baby starts to associate these with going to sleep.

194 - You could introduce changes in the settling routine slowly, week by week. For instance, introduce a lullaby in the first week. In the second week, feed or pat your baby till she falls asleep in your arms while singing the lullaby. In the third week, put her in bed drowsy with the lullaby, then rock or pat her until she falls asleep. The following week, place your hands on your baby, without patting or rocking her. In the final week, put your baby in bed drowsy, still singing the lullaby.

195 - Use a range of settling methods or techniques; don't rely on one particular technique. For settling ideas, turn to 'Find the Quickest Way for Your Baby To Fall Asleep'.

CHAPTER EIGHT

Develop a Sleeping Routine

196 - Whatever sleeping method you are using, all babies benefit from some sort of routine, especially sensitive babies and those who don't like new places and people. A routine helps them predict what is coming next, which makes it easier to get them to sleep.

197 - Start by keeping a sleep log or diary, in which you record the time and duration of all sleeps. See 'A Gift from Me'.

198 - From birth, expose your baby to daylight during the day. This helps him distinguish between day and night, which will result in better sleep at night.

199 - Provide your baby with plenty of opportunities for active floor play, which will tire him out as well as help him master developmental skills.

200 - Stay home as much as possible, especially when establishing a routine.

201 - If you need to go out, plan your outings to fit around your baby's nap times.

202 - Find out what you're more comfortable with: a strict routine with strict, predetermined times of feeding and sleeping, or a more flexible routine.

203 - The simplest routine is feed-play-sleep.

204 - To develop a routine for your baby, use the guidelines below. Be ready to change your routine as your baby grows.

First 6 weeks

Sleep per day: 15 to 18 hours

Nap time: 2 to 4 hours per sleep

Up time: 1 to 1¼ hours

6 weeks to 3 months

Sleep per day: 14 to 15 hours

Nap time: 1½ to 3½ hours per sleep

Up time: 1 to 2 hours

Night-time: 4 to 6 hours

3 to 6 months

Sleep per day: 14 to 15 hours

Nap time: 2-4 sleeps a day, each lasting 1½ to 2½ hours

Up time: 1½ to 2½ hours

Night-time: 4 to 6 hours

6 to 9 months

Sleep per day: 14 to 15 hours

Sleeping time: 2 sleeps a day, each lasting 1½ to 2 hours

Up time: 2 to 3 hours

205 - Here is a sample routine for a six-month old:

- 7am: Wake up, feed
- 9.30am: Nap
- 11.30am: Feed
- 12pm: Play
- 2pm: Nap
- 4pm: Feed
- 4.30pm: Play
- 6.30pm: Bath
- 7pm: Feed, bedtime
- 11pm: Top-up feed (optional)

Find a wide range of daily routines at

http://bit.ly/aVy1oi

206 - Keep to the routine as much as possible, especially in the evening. Don't let your baby be over-handled by friends, siblings, and relatives and delay his sleep time.

207 - Do not change your routine for more than two days in a row. The resulting lack of sleep will make your baby irritable and hard to settle.

208 - Make sure your baby feeds well during the day and gets the bulk of his nutritional needs, to minimize feeding at night. Wake your baby up from naps for a feed, if necessary.

209 - Sensitive, easily distracted babies need quiet feedings during the day, without the distraction of toys and mobiles. When you're out, feed in the car or use the parents' room of a shopping centre.

210 - It's best to feed in dim light. Bright lights are too distracting.

211 - From birth, use the same bedtime ritual every night. This could be a bath, feed, and story before bed.

212 - For most babies, a bath is relaxing but for some babies it may be too stimulating. In that case, bath time can be part of the morning routine.

213 - Avoid boisterous activities just before bedtime.

214 - Turn off the TV or radio at least half an hour before bedtime.

215 - Dim the lights to signal that it is almost time for bed.

216 - Introduce a top-up feed as the last feed of the night, when baby is half asleep, between 10pm and midnight. Hopefully this will last him most of the night without feeding.

217 - At night, only change a very wet or soiled nappy or diaper, and use warm wipes so your baby won't wake up fully.

218 - Keep night feeding sessions short.

219 - If you want to reduce night feeds, reduce your breastfeeding time by two to five mins or give 5ml to 10ml less bottle fed milk at night.

220 - After six months, if your baby has already slept through the night by himself, you could try to offer water and a cuddle instead of a feed.

221 - At night, keep lights low (use a nightlight or small lamp) and don't stimulate baby.

222 - Avoid eye contact, move slowly and try to be as boring as possible.

223 - Don't talk at bedtime, only tell your baby to go asleep repeatedly.

224 - Use the same method to get your baby to sleep for naps as night time.

225 - For naps, put him to sleep in his cot, crib, or bassinet.

226 - Once your baby's routine is established, you can get him used to a variety of places for taking a nap like the stroller, pram, or travel cot so you'll more freedom taking him out.

227 - Wake your baby if his naps are too long.

228 - To wake a baby up during the day:

- open the curtains
- turn on the lights
- remove his blankets
- make noise
- pick up and hold upright
- take off his socks and rub his feet
- unwrap him
- wipe his face with a damp cloth

229 - To get your baby to nap longer, go in when he starts to stir, just before he is completely awake, and use whatever technique to make him fall back asleep. When you do this at each nap time, your baby will eventually have longer naps.

230 - Babies make lots of noises when they're sleeping, and sometimes it may sound like they're awake when they are really still asleep. Recognize your baby's sleeping noises and don't pick him up too quickly.

231 - From eight to 12 weeks, leave your baby in his cot for a short time after waking. This gives him the opportunity to put himself back to sleep.

232 - For long nappers, place the cot or crib in the living room, or wake him after each nap.

233 - For catnappers, encourage a quiet time and play relaxing music.

234 - Make nap time a universal quiet time for the whole family.

235 - When traveling, stick to same bedtime routine. Bring your baby's favorite blanket and/or comfort object and some clips in case the hotel curtains don't close properly.

CHAPTER NINE
Look After Yourself

236 - It is really important to look after yourself when you're struggling with a baby who doesn't sleep much. Remember that you won't be able to look after your baby if you're sleep deprived and unwell.

237 - Accept any help. This is not the time to be polite.

238 - Get your partner to help out as much as possible, for example with:
- cleaning the house
- giving baby a nighttime bottle
- looking after other children
- taking baby out in a sling
- doing shopping
- cooking

239 - Let go of perfection or high standards. Your well-being is more important than a tidy house.

240 - Ask for help from friends, parents, brothers, or sisters, and relatives. You really can't do it all yourself.

241 - Let other children help around the house and call them your 'special helpers'.

242 - Pay for help if necessary, like a cleaner, gardener, handyman, or nanny.

243 - Do your shopping on the Internet and have it home delivered, including your grocery shopping.

244 - Look for a healthy meal service and have meals delivered.

245 - Reward yourself from time to time.

246 - Get out of the house for some 'you' time:
- go shopping
- have a massage, facial, manicure, or pedicure

- visit a friend
- enjoy a nice lunch or dinner

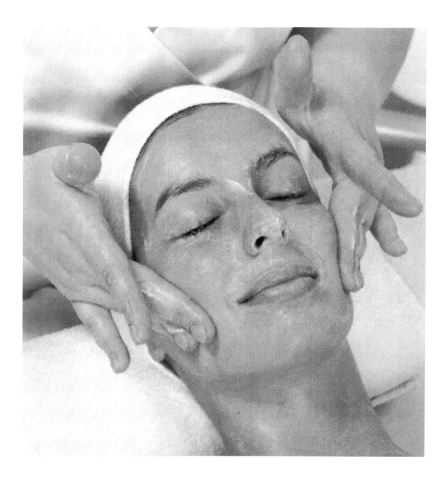

247 - Let someone else hold your baby.

248 - Listen to relaxing music.

249 - Do deep breathing exercises or relaxation techniques.

250 - Meditate.

251 - Play an instrument.

252 - Sing to yourself.

253 - Read a relaxing book, preferably one that has nothing to do with baby care!

254 - Make your own sleep a priority.

255 - Sleep whenever your baby does.

256 - Have power naps. Even a 10-minute nap can give you a boost of energy.

257 - Let older children wait until you've settled the baby.

258 - Get some exercise. Leave your baby with your partner or babysitter while you go to the gym.

259 - Join a mother-and-baby yoga or exercise class.

260 - Get some exercise equipment so you can get fit at home.

261 - Get fit by walking everywhere, pushing your baby in the pram or stroller.

262 - Leave the room when it all gets too much.

263 - Do not feel bad or guilty. You are doing the best you can.

CHAPTER TEN

If Nothing Seems To Work, Don't Despair!

264 - Take a break. Then go back to what you were doing and persist for at least a week, or change your plan completely.

265 - Do what has worked for you in the past.

266 - For a quick fix, try some ideas in 'Find the Quickest Way for Your Baby To Fall Asleep'.

267 - Have reasonable expectations. Night waking is normal for babies aged six to eight months.

268 - Some babies are better sleepers than others, who are easily stressed and need a lot of soothing. This has nothing to do with you. You're not a bad parent.

269 - Put this in perspective: it is only a very short period in your life.

270 - Do not feel guilty. You're doing your best to solve the problem.

271 - Talk about your feelings to your partner, friend, parents, or relatives.

272 - Find support on the Internet. You are bound to find people with issues similar to yours.

273 - Ask your doctor if you can give your baby antihistamines or other types of medication in emergency situations.

274 - Try to see it from your baby's viewpoint. She's tired, she wants to go to sleep but she just doesn't know how. She is definitely not out to make your life difficult!

275 - Seek professional help from a child health nurse, midwife, maternity nurse, lactation consultant, mother-baby unit, doula, or doctor. You could also look for a baby or child sleep clinic in your area - check with your local child health clinic.

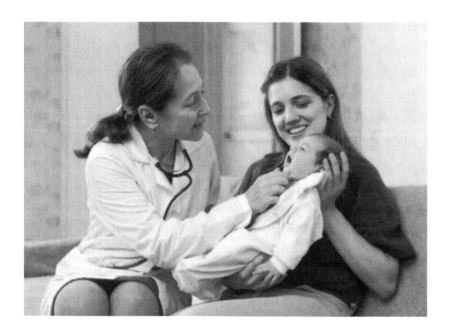

A Gift From Me

Thank you for reading this book. As a token of my appreciation, here are two FREE gifts for you:

- A printable sleep log for keeping a record of your baby's sleep.
- An MP3 recording of waves for you to use as white noise to help your baby fall asleep.

To claim, visit
www.sarahjeffersonbooks.blogspot.com and sign up to my mailing list. You'll also be one of the first to hear when I launch new books.

Enjoy your gifts!
Sarah

Connect with me at:
sarahjeffersonbooks@gmail.com
www.sarahjeffersonbooks.blogspot.com

About the Author

Sarah Jefferson may not be a doctor, nurse, or counselor. But she does know about sleep. Mom of two and insomniac from the day she was born, Sarah is obsessed with sleep - especially baby sleep. She spent many sleepless hours reading whatever she could get her hands on trying to find solutions to get her baby to sleep. Sleep training, crying-it-out, co-sleeping, routines - she's studied and tried them all.

Sarah has successfully helped family and friends with their babies' sleep problems. Now she hopes to share what she's learnt with other parents and carers who are looking for solutions to get their babies to sleep better.

Connect with her at **www.sarahjeffersonbooks.blogspot.com** to find out what she's been up to in her sleepless nights.

Made in the USA
Middletown, DE
01 January 2018